SHATTERING HABITS

Dr. Emma Wagner, DC

Copyright © 2018 Dr. Emma Wagner, DC

All rights reserved.

978-1-7287-2739-4

DEDICATION

Dedicated with love to my 19 year companion and life partner Burton Wagner. Your wisdom and love are a constant support. Thanks to my kids for putting up with all those hours in front of the computer in the writing of this book. Thanks to Sharon Savoy for all of her precious advice, support, and ideas. Thanks to those who helped me edit and get this book into it's final format (for now anyway).

CONTENTS

Dedication	I
Introduction	
Principle 1 – I See What Is	1
Principle 2 – I Choose My Destination	11
Principle 3 – I Am a Spiritual Being on a Physical Journey	17
Principle 4 – I Increase My Adaptability	22
Principle 5 – I Repair My Physical Body	29
Principle 6 – I Change My thoughts, I Change my Life	34
Principle 7 – I Follow Up on Myself	39
Wrapping It All Up	48

Introduction

"Only I can change my life. No one can do it for me."
Carol Burnett

This book is designed for you if:

- You want to take control of your life and health.

- You realize something is not working for you, even if you do not know what it is yet.

- You have reached a plateau in life and want more.

- You want to stop harmful behaviors and thoughts including procrastination, anxiety, depression and/or eating disorders.

- You are seeking a sense of ease and flow.

- You want to gain confidence and self-acceptance.

- You want to take more chances.

- You desire better self-understanding.

- You long for a meaningful life.

Our habits influence everything. They affect how we think, the quality of our relationships, what we do and do not do, our confidence level, and our posture. Earl Nightingale said, "We are all creatures of habit. We can do most things without even thinking about them; our bodies take charge and do them for us."

But what happens when those habits are negative, or our programing runs on its own, and the program doesn't serve us? Examples include childhood fears, lack of confidence carried over from teenage years, and chronic pain from past trauma. We may not even know we have been programed. Our society's cultural norms and our parents set the programs for us, and we can remain unaware of it for years. Most programming happens during childhood when the brain is most impressionable, but it can continue past the age of twenty-five.

I teach a process that shatters your habits, Activates your Life and reprograms your body and mind so that you cannot resume them. The definition of shattering is to weaken, destroy or become insubstantial, which describes the process well. I get clients who come to me at the age of forty-five or seventy, wondering why they are not in control of their life. That is not really what they are complaining about but that really is what is going on, their habits are in control. My clients feel stuck and suffer from procrastination, depression, anxiety, or have physical limitations. Their habits are standing in the way of health, success, and life enjoyment.

My in-office program, which I call a Life Activation, creates inner coherence and organizes the various aspects of your being, allowing them to communicate with each other so they can grow and expand. It enables you to widen your perspective and rewire the body/mind. Finding your authentic self and discovering your genius, by shattering the habits that limited you.

There is so much at stake if you do not find you. You already know why you are on this journey. You understand why it is so important for you to find your true self, your inner magic. German philosopher, Frederick Nietzche once said, "He who has a why can endure anyhow." Your why is essential, as it provides you with the mental energy and motivation to shatter your habits and Activate your Life by stepping outside your comfort zone.

Grant Cardone's book, The 10X Rule, suggests that we have four choices when it comes to taking control of our lives:

1. Do nothing

2. Retreat

3. Take normal levels of action

4. Take massive action – and do so now

Shattering Habits :7 principles to reprograming body and mind is designed to help you take massive action and the necessary steps to reinventing yourself. I recommend that you read it from beginning to end and then focus on each chapter, one by one, in whichever order you prefer. The goal is to implement all the steps, but you can start with the easiest or the most challenging. While you may be familiar with some of the information, I invite you to dive deep into each chapter and challenge yourself. In challenge there is growth.

When I work with clients, we incorporate the principles in this book to reorganize their lives and shatter the habits that lock them into a life they do not want anymore. During each session, we focus on one step and work to break the patterns and anchors held by their mind and body while reinforcing the strategies already learned. The goal is to always create more coherence in life. I explain to my clients that my role is not to fix or change them, but rather to open their perspective to new possibilities and opportunities.

Understanding a concept is not the same as living it. To truly Activate your Life, and ultimately shattering old habits, you need to incorporate both the body and mind. This book will help you understand and achieve more mind/body coherence by doing the exercises included in each step.

Exercise 1: Write down your WHY.

Your WHY is the purpose, cause, or belief that inspires you. Knowing your WHY gives you a filter to make choices at work and at home.

Use these three questions to help you dig deeper:

1. What makes you come alive?

2. What makes you forget to eat and wakes you up in the morning?

3. If you knew you were going to die in one year, what would you do?

Principle 1 – "I see what is"

Are you letting the authentic part of you express itself freely or do you keep it hidden away afraid of what the world will do to it?

I always ask a lot of questions to help my clients understand and evaluate their current situation, understand their habits and what they need help with. Learning about their challenges and what they already implement in their life helps to shed light on whether they are living with the most authentic part of themselves or if they have disconnected from it.

Check in with yourself, allow yourself to see "what is". Even if it is not what you wish to see, even if you are not expressing your authentic self. Auditing yourself is the first step.

Exercise 2: Audit yourself with the Wellness Wheel:

Color in from 0-10 your level of satisfaction in each health area

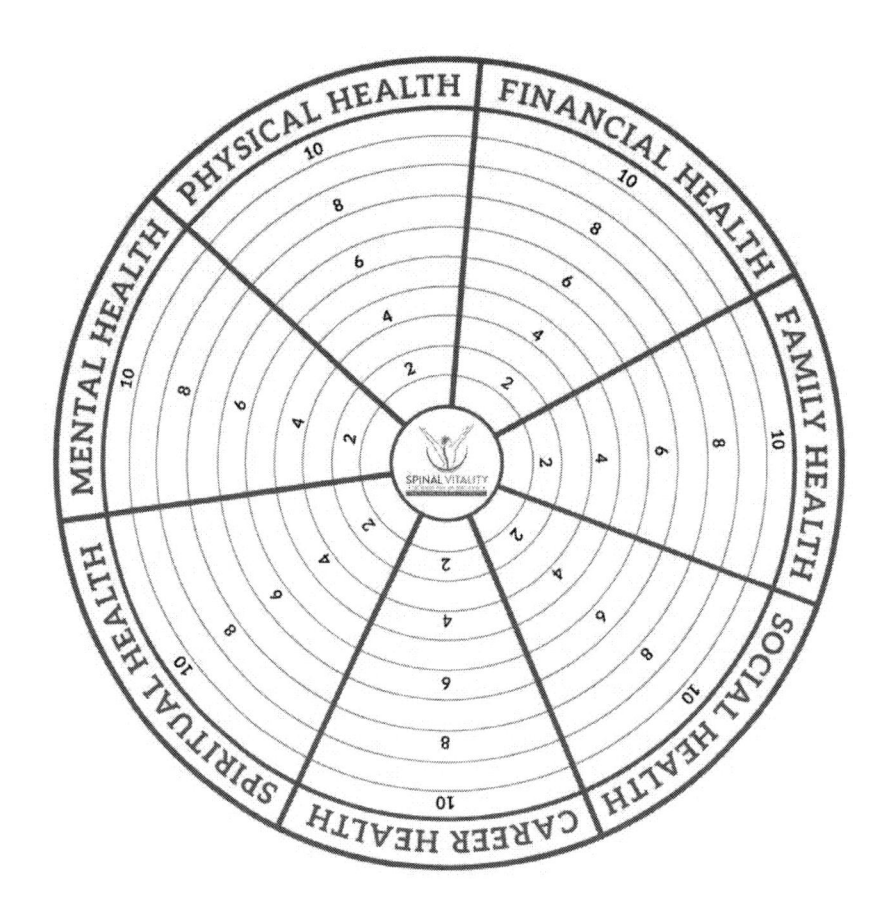

Reflection question: Is your wheel round or does it look like a flat tire?

Auditing ourselves is not an easy process, but you will be more in tune with yourself if you start to listen and reflect. It's about standing in front of the mirror and asking yourself "Is there anything missing?". It is about seeing what needs to be done differently next time and finding the motivation to do it.

There are 3 motivations to allowing your authentic self to be set free:

1. Addressing your suffering and pain.

Pain, both physical and emotional, is really a messenger that something is off in your life. It is a way for our mind-body to say that there is an incoherence: "Stop what you are doing, it is time to do things differently".

Suffering is disconnection from our self, from our life and from what is happening around us. It is the main source of pain. Our society teaches us to avoid this pain and suffering, to just pop a pill and make it go away to continue living a life we are used to.

Procrastination or self-medicating with alcohol or drugs is the first sign that we are suffering, that we are disconnecting ourselves from what is not working for us. When self-medicating is not enough or when we refuse to do it, society tells us to go to the doctor because "we are sick". Between the ages of 14 to 16 years old, my dad (a medical doctor), helped me manage bad headaches by continually prescribing me stronger pills. I needed stronger pills each time which never actually resolved my problems. I feel lucky that from an early age, I learnt that medications were not the solution, but just a way to manage symptoms without addressing the underlying issue.

We can use allopathy (drugs) or green allopathy (herbs and supplements) to get rid of symptoms, killing the messenger without having to address the cause of our suffering – this is how we allow our authentic self to become disconnected. With the evolution of pharmaceuticals, we are finding more drugs on the market are having terrible side effects, and while green allopathy, (taking plants, supplements and essentials oils to manage symptoms) is a better option than taking drugs, it still doesn't allow us to connect with what is going on, to reconnect with our authentic-self suffering within.

With my clients, I explain how our mind creates a paradigm and that paradigm is expressed through our body, where it manifests into reality. Conflict between our personal reality and the societal reality creates tension in the mind-body, leading to disconnection, suffering and pain. With my clients, I read the body and help them discover the source of their disconnection to see the problem for what it is.

By reading the body, I help my clients discover what their true self desires and help them find ways to achieve this. If you are interested in learning more about the messages your body sends you, I would recommend the books the "Inner Cause" by Martin Brofman and "You Can Heal Your Life" by Louise Hay.

Be wary of allowing pain to be your only motivator in finding your authentic self, because when you are not in pain, you will not be seeking who you truly are, what you want, and what you need.

2. Following your Bliss.

Bliss is a powerful motivator in finding your authentic self, but we live in a busy world where it is easy to feel "happy" through superficial means. Let's distinguish between two types of "happiness": one is the transitory emotion of joy and the other is the profound sentiment of happiness. Superficial joy is an immediately rewarding, relatively short-lived experience requiring few or no profound human capacities. Profound bliss involves optimal functioning, using and developing a person's essential abilities to overcome problems and make some progress.

This might not be an easy thing to do, so you might want to start by discovering what doesn't work for you, what makes you feel disconnected, what makes you feel unhappy. The next step would be getting curious and exploring ideas and possibilities to find your bliss. The more you discover what doesn't work for you, the easier it will be to find and follow your bliss.

The Millennials are the generation not willing to settle for a meaningless existence. In my family, my uncle became a role model by following his passion. He was a nurse in France making a good living, but he was not satisfied and didn't find joy in his existence. As a result, he chose to make a change and follow his passion by moving to an island, La Reunion, and becoming a fisherman. He was making less money but became increasingly satisfied living a happier life. I am thankful that in my family, living a happy life was more important than making money.

Some questions to think about:

Do you have a limit to how happy you can be?

Is there a paradigm in your mind that could stop you from being joyful?

Do you have a fear that your tribe would not accept you as one of them if you fully followed your bliss?

"Follow your bliss ... If you do follow your bliss, you put yourself on a kind of track that has been there all the while, waiting for you, and the life that you ought to be living is the one you are living. When you can see that, you begin to meet people who are in your field of bliss, and they open doors to you. I say, follow your bliss and don't be afraid, and doors will open where you didn't know they were going to be." — Joseph Campbell

3. Listening to your inner voice.

All my life there has been an inner voice offering guidance. It started when I was 12 years old, where to kill boredom while driving roads in Africa, I imagined going into the clouds looking for company. I met Max there, my spiritual guide, and since then I use my inner guidance connecting to that presence. I always feel his presence, sometimes gently and sometimes urgently calling for my attention - sometimes I listen and sometimes I do not. The times I find ease the most when connecting to that voice include when I am in a car, when I am walking, when I am meditating and when I am talking myself to sleep.

We live in a world where it is so easy to disconnect from that voice. We are rarely alone and allowing our thoughts to surface, constantly bombarded by TV, radio and other people around us. In order to listen to our inner voice, we need to let it talk to us and allow that inner voice to express itself. At first, you might need to get into a deep state of relaxation for it to happen. There are many practices available that encourage us to do this, including yoga, meditation, Tai Chi, and using a sensory deprivation tank.

Have you heard of Slomo? He is a skater on the San Diego beach path. A video on YouTube titled Slomo tells the story of this former medical doctor. He explains how when he is in slow motion (Slo-Mo) on his skates, his brain shifts, and he gets "in the zone". It is a physiological response where the skater finds his inner peace and guidance. I gained access to those strategies at an early age through the long driving trips. I practiced so often that I created neural-pathways to have easy access to my inner guidance. Practice is what makes it easy for me to connect to my inner guidance now.

Not everyone will hear their inner voice the way they expect to. I met a few people that wanted to experience it but were very frustrated about being unable to hear that voice after a few tries. As unique individuals, we perceive the world in different ways that can be separated into three categories, and this influences how we eventually hear the inner voice:

- **Visual people** use their sight. They will be guided more by light, their ability to see auras, or by written words of guidance that will be there in the world around them.

- **Auditory people** use sounds and will hear the voice within more clearly.

- **Kinesthetic people** will feel their inner voice. I am a kinesthetic and something I had to learn was to transmute what I feel into language.

The more I listen to my inner voice, the easier it is to feel and express it. Network Spinal Analysis (NSA) and Silva Mind Control have been two key techniques that have helped me connect to my inner voice on a deeper level.

I practice NSA, and I would encourage you to look for an NSA practitioner close to you as a great way to connect to that inner voice. Network Spinal Analysis is a chiropractic technique that helps you grow in your self-awareness and learn how to release tension to create a greater experience of connection to yourself and the world around you.

You need to accept and acknowledge what is, in order to move forward, in order to Activate your Life. So, are you ready to explore what is? Are you ready to connect with your authentic self?

*Exercise 3 : **What is my motivation to connect with my authentic self?***

Using our emotions to "see what is":

Emotions are a great way to check in with yourself. Feeling your emotions allows you to see what is and I encourage you to journal them as often as you can.

Emotion is a conscious experience that will create an intense mental activity caused by either pleasure or displeasure. They are triggered by the release of neuropeptides in the body (molecules that regulate a range of functions from reproduction to social behavior) to create a chemical reaction. The molecules influence how the receptors in our cells respond to the environment. I invite you to read Candace Pert's book *"Molecules of Emotions"* to better understand how it functions.

An emotion is always real, it is an instinctive or intuitive feeling that lasts between 30-90 seconds. Once the emotion is felt, the conscious mind acts, and we either use our emotion to continue with our old story (what has been) or to rewrite our story (what could be). Emotions are Energy in Motion (E-Motion), they are energies needed to transform our patterns.

In our society we are taught to think that we are too evolved to get caught up with emotions and that we should be in control of them rather than be controlled *by* them. Young children that easily express their emotions (anger, sadness, or happiness) are taught to suppress them by adults who often find these emotions inappropriate and confusing. Here are 4 helpful tools to help a child or an adult understand and express their emotions in a healthy way:

- Give the feeling a name and encourage talking about the feeling.

- Give an opportunity to identify with that emotion, reflect on what someone else is feeling.

- Learn different ways to respond to specific emotions

    i.e. when I get mad I take a deep breath, count to three and think about the best ways to deal with my problem.

- Give praise and support when expressing emotions and when practicing new ways for expressing them.

Exercise 4: Journal my emotions.

Whenever your mood changes try to write down what you were doing, what you were thinking, and try to match your mood to an emotion or a feeling, don't make a story about it.

By allowing our emotions to be felt and used properly, we give ourselves access to a beautiful and strong energy of transformation. Emotions can help bring awareness to one of our dysfunctional paradigms, allowing us to change our "reality". I see so many people trying to numb their emotions. But when we numb sadness or anger, we also numb happiness and joy. We cannot selectively numb our emotions.

My client Erin had done years of personal growth, she mentioned to me that she sometimes feels "sadness" in her life because she feels lonely. Her training allowed her to feel her sadness and then reason with it, "I am not lonely, I am happily married, I have beautiful kids, a loving family, some friends… no reason to feel sad, really!". And yet sadness came back regularly, as though her mind couldn't convince her body that she had no reason to feel sad. I explained to her that if sadness came back, there was a reason for it, and suggested she put some effort into creating the "community" she craved for. At that instant, tears came to her eyes, and she lit up. I knew that if she put her energy toward creating that community that she needs, her sadness would never come back.

I see this all too often, people spending all their energy to push away what they don't want in their life instead of focusing their energy on creating what they do want. When one sees what is, it is easy to create what we want.

Principle 2- "I choose my destination"

Now that you have figured out where you are and what will motivate you to go further (pain, joy or your inner guidance), it's time to reflect on where you want to go and what you want to create for yourself and for the world. There is only one of you that will ever exist, your uniqueness is a precious gift. Your existence matters, and you are the only one that can make sense of it. The best way to make sense of it is to set goals. Tony Robbins, life coach and philanthropist suggests that "setting goals is the first step in turning the invisible into the visible". By creating new goals, you will define new habits that will take the place of the old habits. For example, by having the goal of being more fit and healthy you will start eating healthier, therefore shattering the habit of eating unhealthily.

There are two types of goals that are important to set:

1. Dream goals:

Dream goals are about the destination, not the journey. Dream goals are about the summit, the 'nut', the ideal outcome. By setting a goal that is currently out of your reach but makes your heart bubble and your energy expand, it will fuel your dreams and bring you close to it.

The dream goal doesn't need to be SMART (see SMART goals). You don't need to know if you will ever be able to achieve it, or when or what it will take to get there or even if it is impossible or outside of your zone of comfort.

"The only limit to the height of your achievements is the reach of your dreams and your willingness to work for them."– Michelle Obama

To make a dream goal: dream big - just you, a pad, a pen and your thoughts.
Don't think of any ideas as too outlandish or foolish—remember—you're dreaming! Let the thoughts fly and take careful notes. Make a list of what you want to Be, to Do and to Have. Allow yourself two hours to dream big and put on paper in these 3 columns your dreams. Over the next few days, write down more dream goals on your list. Read it one last time and then forget your list in a drawer for a few months or a few years.

*Exercise 5: **What is your Dream goal?** If you were to dream big and shoot for the stars, what would this look like? Take a couple of hours and fill in everything you want to be, to do and to have.*

I want to be:	I want to do:	I want to have:

2. SMART goals:

Keep your dream goals in mind when you set your SMART goals and start taking actions on your SMART goals.

SMART goals are Specific -A specific goal has a much greater chance of being accomplished than a general goal. To set a specific goal you must answer the six "W" questions:

Who: Who is involved?

What: What do I want to accomplish?

Where: Identify a location.

When: Establish a time frame.

Which: Identify requirements and constraints.

Why: Specify reasons, purpose or benefits of accomplishing the goal.

EXAMPLE: A general goal would be "Get in shape.", but a specific goal would be "Join a health club and workout 3 days a week."

SMART goals are Measurable - Establish concrete criteria for measuring progress towards the attainment of each goal you set. When you measure your progress, you stay on track, reach your target dates, and experience the exhilaration of achievement that spurs you on to continued effort required to reach your goal. To determine if your goal is measurable, ask questions such as:

How much? How many? How will I know when it is accomplished?

SMART goals are Attainable – They are based on your abilities, interests, needs, and desires. For example, when choosing a career goal, you should consider your skills and interests. Goals that may have seemed far away and out of reach eventually move closer and become attainable, not because your goals shrink, but because you grow and expand to match them.

SMART goals are Realistic- To be realistic, a goal must represent an objective towards which you are both *willing* and *able* to work. Do not set goals because you think you "should" or because they "sound good." Look at your life and the direction you want it to take – set goals that seem realistic, but more importantly, pick goals that you **want** to achieve. A goal can be both high and realistic, you are the only one who can decide just how high your goal should be.

SMART goals are Time-bound – A goal should be grounded within a time frame. With no time frame tied to it, there is no sense of urgency. If you want to create more health in your life, a good goal can be: "I will pack my lunch from home 3 days this week rather than eating out."

SMART goals are becoming more and more common in personal and professional life. You can Google it to get more help in setting your SMART goals.

"People with goals succeed because they know where they're going." - Earl Nightingale

Key point: **No one likes to lose.** Our mind can't focus on goals of having less or losing something. If your goal is to lose weight or to have less pain it won't work, or it will be very hard to accomplish. Instead, think about why you want to lose weight: to be healthier, to fit into and look good in a sexy dress, to get more positive attention, to have more energy. Or why you want to have less pain: to enjoy life more, to play with the grandkids, to have more energy. Choose the one that matters most to you as your goal.

I was able to lose weight (I lost a total of 18lbs) by focusing on eating to feed my feminine power, to have more creativity and intuition.

Exercise 6: My first SMART goal is:

Is it Specific?

How much? How many? How will I know when it is accomplished?

Is it attainable?

Is it realistic?

Is it time bound?

Principle 3: "I am a spiritual being on a physical journey"

Recognizing that we are more than a physical being is a key principle in shattering our bad habits and activating our life. We are energy beings as well as physical beings. You can experience this "energy" when you walk into a room of people or when you cross someone on the street, and you can sense attraction or repulsion towards them. It is not something physical and it has nothing to do with how they look. It is deeper, a "feeling" you have in the core of your being. Some people are more sensitive to it whereas others can dismiss it more easily. Have you ever paid attention to those sensations? You might already recognize that there is much more than the physical reality and want to experience more depth, excited to play to the fullest in life.

There is a space or field between us all. Scientists used to believe that the universe is made of atoms. Now we understand that it is a field of energy, information, and consciousness. This field affects us even if we are not aware of it.

Understanding that you are an energetic being, first and foremost, is an important step in your journey toward freedom. If you want to get more, give more, learn more and experience more, then being curious and willing to go beyond the physical body is a big part in the journey of living the full human experience. Learn to master your full potential and make a bigger difference in your world.

Our bodies, especially our nervous systems, are the interface with the field. We have the ability to influence the field as well as be influenced by it. It shapes our lives, our bodies, our experiences and our relationships, as we shape it. The field is where magic, science, and the sacred meet.

Buddha said "when the student is ready, the teacher will appear." There are many different types of practitioners that work with energy, and you can find them everywhere. Be curious, it is fun to explore our spiritual side.

Reiki is a Japanese technique. The word Reiki is made of two Japanese words - Rei which means "God's Wisdom or the Higher Power" and Ki which is "life force energy". So, Reiki is actually "spiritually guided life force energy." Practicing Reiki is tapping into an unlimited supply of "life force energy" to improve one's health and enhance the quality of life. There are Reiki practitioners all over the world and the beauty of Reiki healing is that it can be given and received even if the client and practitioner aren't in the same room. Why? Because the power of intention causes energy to flow to where it's most needed.

Acupuncture practitioners are also very accessible, though the clients do need to be in the physical presence of the needles. This modality stimulates the flow of chi (life force energy) to rebalance the body. Originating in ancient China, acupuncture is now widely practiced in the West. It is linked to the belief that disease is caused by disruptions to the flow of energy, or chi, in the body and stimulates points on or under the skin called acupuncture points or acupressure points to release this chi. The chi then travels through channels called meridians to restore healthy body function.

Reflexology is another modality that frees up blocked energy and promotes healing by stimulating the meridians, organs, and organ systems through points on the feet, hands, and ears. Reflexology (or foot reflexology) is a therapy based on the principle that there are small and specific areas of innervations in the hands and feet that correspond to specific muscle groups or organs of the body. In this system, the nerve endings in the extremities provide a "map" to stimulate the rest of the body.

Chakras Healing refers to creating a balance. Chakras are the seven energy centers in the body which house our mental and emotional strength. Starting at the base of the spine, they run vertically all the way to the crown of the head. Balancing the chakras restores a harmonious flow of energy throughout the body. The effect of well-balanced chakras often translates into a feeling of well-being, relaxation, centeredness, increased vitality and embodiment of oneself. The most common practices you can use to balance your chakras include hands-on energy healing, meditation, and breath work.

In my chiropractic practice, I utilize a hands-on technique accessing the universal energy or Chi, the Chakras and spinal gateways (an energetic bridge between your physical and energy body) to remove interference and allow the mind-body communication to flow with ease.

The energy field, as I understand it, is constructed of 4 basic layers:

1. The Lifeforce layer helps to maintain normal body functions.

2. The Emotional layer helps to express our emotions.

3. The Mental layer helps to engage our thought processes.

4. The Soul layer is our direct connection with others, the world, and God.

These 4 layers can either be energy rich or energy poor. If they are energy-rich, it is going to be easy to use the resources from those fields in our life whereas if they are energy poor, it will be necessary to find energy elsewhere to use those resources. If all are depleted, moving through life will be rather challenging. My role is to create coherence between these layers and the body, assuring my clients that they have access to energy in all aspects of their life.

Understanding and working with your energy body to create coherence will allow you to Activate Your Life with ease.

Exercise 7: 3 actions to start your self-discovery journey.

1. Set an Intention: "I want to learn more about myself beyond my physical body". Consciously acknowledging your desire to learn more is like opening a door and setting your journey in motion.
My intention is: _____

_____

_____

2. Learn about other people's beliefs: Read, have discussions, experience awe inspiring places … to experience that life is more than your day to day routine. I enjoy reading Wayne Dyer, Paolo Coelho and The Dali Lama to name a few. This year I visited the vortexes in Sedona, AZ, the Japanese garden in San Francisco, CA and the Meditation garden at the Self-Realization temple in San Diego, CA. One that is on my bucket list is the Chartres's Cathedral in France. There are many places, churches, temples, gardens around the world for us to explore and learn from.

Make a list of the book, the movies and the places you hear about and that picks your curiosity:

3. Watch for signs.

As you cultivate a spiritual practice, you may find that the universe sends you little nudges or clues to encourage you on your journey. You may begin to notice strange coincidences or undeniable signs that lead you deeper into your spiritual journey. It may be something as simple as having three different people recommend the same book or connecting with a kindred spirit through a seemingly random occurrence.

Journal the coincidences in your life:

Principle 4: "I increase my adaptability"

It is not uncommon that we get burned out from life. Sometimes we can't even imagine moving forward, and the idea is merely to survive another day, so shattering our old way of life sounds like too much work. Our energy and our stamina is spent. Life has thrown too much "crap" at us.

In 2012, I was there. Juggling my practice, my two kids that were seven and ten at that time, and my husband who was having a hard time with life, I was overwhelmed and pretty sure that the end of the world was coming. My dreams were filled with "end of the world" scenarios, the Mayan's calendar announced it. I had read and watched fantasy books and movies picturing it. I was at the end of my rope. I remember telling myself that if the world didn't end 12/12/12, I had to start living again and not just "survive."

Our mind-body's resilience has limits and it will slowly break down if we don't nurture it. We were designed to be extremely resilient but not indestructible. Our nervous system has developed over thousands of years to be very effective in either fighting for survival or thriving.

Have you ever heard about the autonomic nervous system?

The autonomic nervous system is the part of our nervous system that is responsible for the regulation of our unconscious bodily functions such as heart rate, digestion, respiratory rate, and sexual arousal. It is divided into two parts, the sympathetic and the parasympathetic nervous system.

The sympathetic division, located mainly in the mid back, prepares the body for defense situations—fight, flight or hide. A highly activated sympathetic system modifies our posture (defense posture), increases heart rate and the force of each heartbeat, increases our breathing rate and releases stored energy to the muscles for running or fighting. Not only that, but the sympathetic system slows body processes that are less important in emergencies, such as digestion and healing.

The parasympathetic division, located in the neck and pelvis, is the antagonist of the sympathetic nervous system; its job is to heal and grow. It slows the heart rate and decreases blood pressure, it stimulates the digestive tract to process food and eliminates waste allowing energy from the processed food to be used to restore and build tissues.

In our busy society, our sympathetic nervous system is too often stimulated, and we don't give much opportunity to the parasympathetic nervous system to do its job of restoring and rejuvenating us. We live in a culture of pushing our mind-body to the ultimate limit and not allowing it time to rest. We don't feed it the food it needs and add to our stress by keeping ourselves busy, always pushing forward and trying to fulfill every expectation everyone has of us. I know I am exaggerating, or at least I hope I am.

You can think of your adaptability like a credit card account. Let's say you were given $1,000,000 in your adaptability account when you were created in your mom's womb (you know when Mr. Spermatozoid met Mss. Ovule). Some moms already tapped into your account when they don't take care of themselves well during pregnancy. We now know that expecting moms can't drink alcohol, can't smoke, need to exercise, relax, feel joy, and be excited about their baby's arrival. Sometimes the birth is traumatic for the baby, such as a C-section, forceps, or a prolonged labor. My first born was born by C-section after 16hrs of intense painful labor and believe me, it was not my choice, he was just a big baby (4.4kg). Knowing about his adaptability account I took measures to replenish it within hours of his birth, a chiropractic adjustment.

Everything that we do after conception will affect that adaptability account one way or another.

C-section -$50k, Gentle regular chiropractic care +$10k, breastfeeding +$20k, bottle feeding -$20k, fall on the head -$50k, vaccinations, the absence of love or sleeping on daddy… everything counts.

By the time I see my clients, that adaptability account has been depleted. The banker (the mind) starts to notice that too much has gone out and not enough has come in. It starts to keep your spending to a minimum because it knows that with your lifestyle, you are running out too fast. This is when symptoms (messages from your body) start to occur and you look for help. Most people start by taking drugs to help them cope with the symptoms so that they can continue to live the life that creates the symptoms. It is like refusing to replenish the account and taking a second credit card.

So how do we replenish our adaptability account?

Our body has a natural pharmacy within that is far more advanced and efficient to replenish our adaptability account than the drugs the pharmaceutical companies create.

There are 3 factors that are vital for us to have access to our natural pharmacy:

1. Nutrition:

A whole food diet that is rich in nutrients is the foundation. It is important that the fruit and vegetables don't spend too much time in a cold chamber to maintain their nutrient value. Better yet, grow your own food, have fruit trees, or just some fresh herbs in your kitchen. Try to buy local produce from a local producer and focus on quality rather than quantity. So much of the fruit and veggies we find in supermarkets were harvested when they were still green and have spent lots of time in cold chambers, leading to them being depleted in nutrients. You also want to stay away from packaged and processed foods that are just empty calories, loaded with sugar and trans-fats which are responsible for diseases such as diabetes and high cholesterol. Remember the foods you eat are the building blocks for creating new cells, new tissues and allowing your body to function at its best. You are what you eat!

Would you put dirty gas in your car? Food in your body is no different.

There are many healthy options available and the key is to understand your body and find the best diet for you. Remember that each one of us is unique, it is called bio-individuality. It is not because something works for your neighbor that it will work for you.

In my office, I like using muscle testing and blood work to help my clients figure out what easy changes they can make in their diet to replenish their adaptability account. Food sensitivities and gut health are important determining factors for creating your ideal diet. An elimination diet with slow reintroduction of common trigger foods will help you learn how food affects your body. Understand that sometimes it is not the food but all the pesticides and other chemicals in contact with our food that is the real problem.

2. Exercise:

Regular exercise is one of the best things you can do for your adaptability account. It has many benefits, including improving your overall health and fitness, and reducing your risk for many chronic diseases. Exercises increase blood flow around the body, allowing our natural pharmacy to release the organic medicine into our bloodstream.

There are many different types of exercise; it is important that you pick a combination of them:

   - Endurance or aerobic activities increase your breathing and heart rate. They keep your heart, lungs, and circulatory system healthy and improve your overall fitness. Examples include brisk walking, jogging, swimming, and biking.

   - Strength or resistance training exercises make your muscles stronger which is very important for bone density. Some examples are lifting weights and using a resistance band.

   - Balance exercises are key to all functional movement. They help your postural equilibrium, muscular balance, joint dynamics, brain function and fall prevention. Balance training is important because balance is a part of everything we do. To improve your balance, try tai chi or exercises like standing on one leg.

   - Flexibility exercises stretch your muscles and can help your body stay limber. Yoga and doing various stretches can make you more flexible. Stretching is the forgotten exercise and yet it is a very important one to do, make sure to stretch because your body needs it. Increasing body flexibility increases our mental flexibility as well.

The best exercise for you is the one you will do regularly. I recommend that you exercise in a way that will incorporate a little of these four types of exercises.

3. Stimulating our Parasympathetic Nervous System (PNS):

Remember that our physiology can function in two different states, a state of rest and healing directed by the parasympathetic nervous system and a state of defense directed by the sympathetic nervous system. To heal and regenerate our mind-body, we need to allow our body time for it.

Here are the activities that stimulate the parasympathetic nervous system:

- Take rest days and be sure to sleep for 7-8 hours a night.

- Mind-body centered exercises such as yoga or tai chi, or light to moderate aerobic exercise such as walking or swimming for at least 30 minutes.

- Meditation & Massage. Stress relief and relaxation are hugely impactful in stimulating the parasympathetic mode.

- Deep breathing exercises.

- Singing and gargling are 2 ways to stimulate the vagus nerve which activates the parasympathetic system.

Key point: The Parasympathetic Nervous System has a direct effect on our adaptability account and achieving optimal wellness. My favorite tool that I use with my clients and strongly recommend is Network Spinal Analysis (NSA) for its ability to allow your body to shift to a state of relaxation, growth, and healing.

Exercise 8 : track your actions weekly that increase your adaptability.

		Food	Water	Exercise	PNS
Monday		B_____ L_____ D_____ S_____	💧💧💧💧 💧💧💧💧		
Tuesday		B_____ L_____ D_____ S_____	💧💧💧💧 💧💧💧💧		
Wednesday		B_____ L_____ D_____ S_____	💧💧💧💧 💧💧💧💧		
Thursday		B_____ L_____ D_____ S_____	💧💧💧💧 💧💧💧💧		
Friday		B_____ L_____ D_____ S_____	💧💧💧💧 💧💧💧💧		
Saturday		B_____ L_____ D_____ S_____	💧💧💧💧 💧💧💧💧		
Sunday		B_____ L_____ D_____ S_____	💧💧💧💧 💧💧💧💧		

Principle 5: "I repair my physical body"

The idea is to repair the damage that has been done to our bodies by years of repetitive stress (habits) or by a traumatic event like a car accident or fall. Like the vast majority of people, you probably don't realize when your body is in a state of pseudo-dysfunction until it is too late. You work out a few times a week, try to eat healthy, and avoid drugs. All of that being said, you probably think you're pretty healthy until you throw out your back picking a pen up off the floor – true story, one of my first client, retired football player. Or your twist your ankle stepping off the curb and it start a serie of injuries. Once you notice one dysfunction in your body, you'll start noticing many, many more. It's all interconnected, and you'll start realizing that things like your feet being turned out when you walk, your head not turning as far while you drive, or the chronic tightness in your lower back, are all symptoms of a body in distress. It's all connected.

Get checked regularly by a holistic practitioner, we all have our specialties. Being a holistic chiropractor myself, my preference goes to holistic chiropractors. But any holistic health care professional can help you repair your physical body, as your body has amazing capacities to repair itself.

1. The brain: The brain is the control center of the body. No matter how your brain is functioning today, you are not stuck with the brain you have and can rewire it to make it function at a higher level. Our brain can repair itself, it is called brain plasticity. At any age, we can make improvements to better our brain function. There is an older lower brain responsible for basic bodily processes such as respiration, movement, and regulating emotions (especially hunger and fear), and a newer higher brain that is responsible for higher-level cognitive functions such as sensation, voluntary movement, thought and memory. We need to access our higher brain function to fully Activate our Lives and reprogram ourselves.

Here are the 7 proven ways to rewire your brain, shattering old habits and Activating your Life:

1. Get Plenty of Sleep – sleep is like a mini detox for the brain.

2. Reduce Stress – stress kills existing neurons.

3. Reduce Alcohol Intake – alcohol also kills off brain cells.

4. Eat healthily – our brain consumes 20% of all nutrients we eat, be sure to include flavonoids and omega 3's.

5. Do something new – this creates new brain pathways, increasing your intelligence.

6. Exercise regularly – exercise is good for everything!

7. Be curious and question everything – it forces your brain to innovate and create new pathways.

My husband and I understand the importance of having a healthy functioning brain. All our programs at Spinal Vitality, The Healthy Brain&Body Center, revolve around proper brain function. We look at balancing the right and left side of the brain, at the neurotransmitters (little molecules helping in the communication), and at how the different parts of the brain communicate with each other and the body.

2. The gut: Naturopathic doctors, nutrition-oriented chiropractors, functional medicine practitioners and nutritionists are your best allies to implement the four R's of gut repair:

R = Remove the foods that are causing inflammation. The most common irritants are gluten, dairy, soy and processed foods. With my clients, I use muscle testing and blood work to determine what foods are causing inflammation. There are natural ways to harmonize our body with foods so that they don't irritate and inflame the gut anymore. NAET practitioners specialize in harmonizing food allergies and sensitivities.

R = Replace the nutrients that are required for digestion to take place. This includes improving stomach acid and digestive enzymes. The idea is to support digestion while the gut heals. You can think of this step as doing everything you can to support your digestion – and it will vary from person to person. Many people will do well by adding more raw vegetables and fruit to their diet which are naturally enzyme-rich, while others with severely compromised digestion may have to avoid raw foods and only eat their fruits or vegetables well-cooked or blended.

R = Reinoculate the good bacteria. Our intestinal tracts are host to over 500 different types of bacteria. In fact, you might be surprised to know that you have more bacteria in your gut than cells in your body! This step involves replenishing the gut with healthy bacteria using supplemental probiotics and/or fermented foods such as kefir, kimchi, sauerkraut, and miso, which are all naturally rich in probiotics. These microorganisms that live in our gut are helpful in aiding digestion and nutrient absorption.

R = Repair. Once your diet is in check and stressors eliminated (or at least limited), you can begin to repair the damage done and work at regenerating the lining of your gut with specific nutrients—Be aware that this can take up to six months.

3. Posture: Posture is a habit. Good posture isn't just about looks. How we sit, stand, and walk affects both our health and our moods. Look at some photos of how you stand

and sit. Is your head over your shoulders or way out in front? Are your shoulders over your hips? Do your hips and ankles line up? Are your shoulders and hips level? By understanding proper posture, you can learn about your own postural deviations and determine which corrective exercises will work best to improve your alignment. So, stop slouching and get centered with these 5 posture tips.

- Test your posture and learn to stand properly.

- Work on your core strength – yoga is a great way.

- Correct your posture in every situation – sleeping, sitting and standing.

- Hold your phone and tablet keeping your head on your shoulders.

- Do posture-correcting exercises.

I regularly recommend this simple exercise: once per hour sit or stand straight by placing your head on top your shoulders, your shoulders on top of your hips, and tighten your abs. Take a deep breath in and then release the breath by squeezing your shoulder blades together – repeat three times every hour. If you are unable to position yourself on your own, work with a chiropractor or a personal trainer that has knowledge in postural rehabilitation.

4. Organs: According to Traditional Oriental Medicine, every organ in your body has a repair/maintenance schedule on a daily basis. The more you know about your body and its rhythms, the easier it is to maintain your health. Our organs have the ability to regenerate themselves once the stressors are removed and the dysfunction is corrected. I use TBM (Total Body Modification), a chiropractic technique that uses muscle testing to diagnose and correct organ imbalance by reconnecting communication between the organ and the brain. Other great resources are an acupuncturist or a functional medicine practitioner.

5. Organ Systems: Not only do the organs need to work on their own, but they also need to work within their system. For example, the digestive system includes the stomach, the intestines, the liver, the gallbladder and the pancreas. They all need to work together for a healthy digestive system.

We have fantastic, intelligent bodies that when given what they need, can repair themselves. We just need to focus our attention and energy on what those needs are.

Exercise 9: Get a full body holistic checkup- what did you learn about yourself?

Principle 6 "I change my thoughts, I change my life"

"I can't change the direction of the wind, but I can adjust my sails to always reach my destination." - Jimmy Dean.

We all know how happy, optimistic and positive thoughts create a spring in our step and spur us into action. The three pillars of a healthy mind are optimism, flexibility and curiosity. But it is not that easy to change our thought process and shatter our habits, if it was, everyone would do it and the world would be a different place.

In order to change our thoughts, the first thing to do is to **gain knowledge** and to be prepared. "Knowledge is power". You don't know what you don't know and what you don't know can still hurt you.

In today's world of internet, audiobooks, and Ted talks, gaining knowledge is easy. I have a friend who teaches yoga and she is so inspiring. Every time someone in her class mentions a condition, an illness or a problem that she doesn't know much about, she goes to the used bookstore or thrift store and buys a $1 book about that subject. She has gained a lot of knowledge over her 15 years of practice.

The two main challenges are not to be overwhelmed, because we often look for information on a subject when it has created a stress in our life (cancer, diabetes etc), and we need to learn to be critical of the information we are reading as there are two sides to every story. When you search for information, remember that everyone is unique and what works for one person will not necessarily work for all. There is not one magic pill!

A good way to check on the information is to look for who is presenting the information and if there might be a hidden agenda or a conflict of interest. For example, the guidelines offered by the American Heart Society is financed by big agricultural lobbies that are more interested in their bottom line than in your health. Their guidelines are out of proportions in terms of grains, fruits, veggies and fats for a truly healthy diet. Develop a curious and critical mind by looking at both sides of the story and decide what makes the most sense for you.

The second thing to do is to **listen to both the ego and the soul.** We have two guiding voices, our soul guidance voice and our challenging ego voice.

The ego was described by Sigmund Freud as a part of our psyche. It is the image we have of ourselves, our social mask, our titles and roles. Everyone has one and must live with it, but you don't have to believe and limit yourself by it. The ego voice will tell you "Once everything falls into place, I'll feel peace. I am a victim of circumstances. I am not good enough. I am better than everyone else, etc…". The ego is not bad, it just gives you a narrow perspective of life. It is not about turning off the ego voice, but instead acknowledge that voice and say, "you are right I am not good enough yet, show me what I can do to better myself". It's about asking our soul voice, which is a source of unconditional love, courage and strength to step in and guide us. There is a natural tension between the soul and ego, when there is tension between two sides the best way to resolve it is with dialogue. Let both sides have their say. Communication is less about talking and more about listening. When we listen to both voices we can find peace and understanding rather than conflict. Communication is key!

"Communication leads to community, that is, to understanding, intimacy and mutual valuing." - Rollo May.

Consciously working towards fulfilling both our sole purpose and our need to empower our identity is a key to Activating our Life. The key, in dark moments, is to recognize that we are unique and amazing individuals. There are moments where I feel depressed, where I feel awkward or not enough. In those moments, I ask the voice inside how I can better myself to make this world better.

Here are a few tips to help balance communication between ego and soul:
- Realize that everyone has an ego and that yours is one in an ocean of egos.
- Allow your soul to empower your ego. Honestly think, feel and say, "I am Enough"

- Use your ego to serve itself and others. "As we let our own light shine, we unconsciously give other people the right to do the same." - Nelson Mandela.
- Cultivate a playful soul. Playfulness opens us up to our own unique creativity and capacity for personal fulfillment.
- Recognize that things are constantly changing. Enlightenment, like health, is not an end goal but a constant pursuit. Allow yourself to keep on learning and growing.

The last aspect to changing our thoughts is to **rewire our brain**. We are creatures of habit because our subconscious minds are responsible for 90-95% of our behaviors. We were brainwashed into believing that things are the way they are because they just are. No more, no less. It is vital to rewire our brains to change our habits. Luckily our brains can change, neuroscientists call it brain plasticity: the brains ability to change, evolve and create new connections.

In growing up, our brains got wired a certain way based on our life experiences. There were rules to follow and expectations to be met. Not meeting those expectations leads to disappointing others, disappointing others leads to disappointing yourself, being disappointed in yourself leads to self-doubt, self-doubt leads to insecurity, insecurity leads to uncertainty, uncertainty leads to unhappiness, and unhappiness sucks the fun out of life. A vicious cycle. And thank goodness that we can rewire our brains and create a glorious cycle instead.

So, what would it take for you to create a glorious cycle for yourself?

We have trillions of brain cells, resulting in thousands (if not millions) of connections correlating with habits in every area of our life. Donald Hebb's landmark discovery in 1949 suggested that "neurons that fire together wire together", this best explains the process of connecting and strengthening brain pathways. The key is to activate as many of these pathways as possible since they work synergistically together. One pathway alone is not enough to successfully rewire your brain. However, when you repeatedly align your beliefs, feelings, vision, and actions you will experience lasting changes in your brain.

This means that you need to visualize your new outcome and use as many of your senses as possible to make it concrete. Try to really feel the "feelings" you will have in the new outcome, make the colors vivid in your mind, use smells, touch and any other physical sensation you can to engage your brain in wiring this new pathway.

<u>Key points:</u>

- Your brain can change when you are alert, engaged, motivated and ready to act.
- Initial changes are temporary, so repeat, repeat, repeat.
- Emotions are a key factor in rewiring your brain, review step one of this book to remember the power and reality of emotions.

Exercise 10: Identify a belief and create an affirmation that you want to imprint in your brain.

ie: Today is the best day of the rest of my life. Everything I do turns out exquisitely better that I could have ever planned. I am extremely confident. People want to be with me, they want to know what I know and do what I do….

Make a few copies of your affirmation. Read your affirmation as you wake up and at night just before you fall asleep. Have copies of your affirmation on your bathroom mirror, on your fridge, on your computer, or in your car so that it gets imprinted at multiples times every day. Use your emotions and be excited, happy, enthusiastic when reading your affirmation and see it coming to life.

Principle 7 – "I follow up on myself"

This last step is probably the most important one, and often the most forgotten.

In business, it is well known that the money is in the follow up. If you don't follow up with people you meet (at networking events, trade shows, fairs, etc) then you are wasting the time, energy, money and effort that you put into meeting them in the first place!

The same is true in your personal life: if you don't have a system to follow up with yourself, you are wasting your time, energy, money and effort. When you are following up on yourself:

- Learn to recognize the season you are in.
- Use synchronicities to get the best of life.
- Celebrate your wins to wire your brain for success.

1. Recognizing the season you are in:

Looking back at our own life is so interesting. Have you ever wondered what steps and actions have brought you to where you are today? Have you looked at what seeds you have planted, and cared for? Have they flourished?

Maybe you never felt like you planted any seeds in your life. Maybe you have, but never cared for them long enough to have them flourish. If you have ever tried growing a garden, you know it takes time, the need to respect the seasons, and regular care.

There are seasons in life similar to the seasons of the year:

    - <u>Springs</u> are the springboard to getting where you want to go. It is the beginning of a wondrous world and a life full of new adventures. In Spring, we like to rediscover the world being reborn around us. It is a time of learning and of gaining knowledge, just as a newborn who takes in sights and sounds for the first time. There is so much to discover, it is a time where opportunities arise.

    - In <u>summers</u>, we continue to grow and transform, just as from the beautiful flowers, fruits are born. This is a time where we can reap some of the benefits of our crops. As well as being a time of joy and comfort, it is also a time to be careful of our responsibilities and of managing our resources and energy properly. The seeds we planted have transformed under our care into the foundation of our being, allowing us to become our own person, responsible for our own life, making our own decisions and determining what sort of person we will be.

    - <u>Falls</u> are the most productive time of life. This is the time when all of our labors come into fruition, and we store away the resources that will sustain us through the winter. In fall, we are established in some career, profession, or other work, and we have a routine. We have gained valuable experience that enables us to guide and direct both ourselves and others who may work with us toward better and more productive work. As you gear up for another winter, it is the best time to take full responsibility of what happened in the previous seasons, both good and bad. This is the time where you can open yourself to learning the lessons that the previous seasons taught you and put everything into perspective. Only by doing so can you be ready once more to handle another winter and plan for the following spring & summer.

- <u>Winters</u> always come. Of course, we have to be ready for it, so we are not stuck in the cold without a coat. When winter comes, life slows down, and we can become retrospective as well as introspective. We have time to cherish our families. It is a time to focus on the ultimate meaning of our life, and to enjoy the *spiritual* fruits of all our labors. It is a time to start planning what will be the next seeds we are going to plant. Be ready to appreciate the winters in your own life, take time to regenerate your energy for the next spring.

<u>Key points:</u>

- Recognize your season and what season you need to be in.

- Be patient with your life as time will change, and a new season will come.

- Recognize in life that seasons don't last the same amount of time.

I am always anxious at the end of winter, stirring new ideas in my head and preparing to plant many seeds. During springs, I don't always nurture all of the seeds I planted, leaving some seeds uncared for (on the back burner). I recognize that timing is key and focusing on the seeds that advance me to my goals (Step #2) is essential. During Falls, I settle into my routine and enjoy the fruits of my work. Saving my harvest to enjoy the quiet of winter with my family until I am ready to plant more seeds, and the cycle goes on. Do you know the story of **The Ant and the Grasshopper** by Aesop?

The Ant and the Grasshopper by Aesop-
One bright day in late autumn a family of Ants were bustling about in the warm sunshine, drying out the grain they had stored up during the summer, when a starving Grasshopper, his fiddle under his arm, came up and humbly begged for a bite to eat.

"What!" cried the Ants in surprise, "haven't you stored anything away for the winter? What in the world were you doing all last summer?"

"I didn't have time to store up any food," whined the Grasshopper; "I was so busy making music that before I knew it the summer was gone."

The Ants shrugged their shoulders in disgust.

"Making music, were you?" they cried. "Very well; now dance!" And they turned their backs on the Grasshopper and went on with their work.

The process of a Life Activation helps bring you into the season of Spring. It is an ideal process when you find yourself in Spring or the need to be in Spring.

Exercise 11 :
What season are you in? _____

What season would you like to be in? _____

2. The concept of synchronicity.

Does life just happen to you? Are you a victim, pushed around by life? Or does life happen through you? Are you your own master, in control of your destiny?

Synchronicity is a concept first introduced by analytical psychologist Carl Jung, that suggests events are "meaningful coincidences" if they occur with no causal relationship yet seem to be meaningfully related. More simply, this means that everything in the universe is intimately connected, and that there must exist a collective unconscious of humankind so that events happening all over the world at the same time must be connected in some unknown way.

I long ago stopped believing in coincidence and started to look for synchronicity. To make synchronicities arise more often in my life, to pay attention to the magic and to learn to access it. I love looking back at my life now and seeing all of the "divine intervention" that took place in it and how one thing led to another.

A couple of personal examples:
- When I graduated high school, I was uninterested in studying. Partying and having fun were my number one priorities. I knew my parents would not let me get away with not going to college. In France, a few months before graduation you must fill out a "wish list" to will determine your future schooling. I thought about the different subjects I liked in school that seemed easy and low key. Chemistry came to mind right away, so that was my first choice. I had to write in a minimum of two curriculum. Looking at the booklet they gave us, biochemistry caught my eye. I remember thinking chemistry and biochemistry must be very similar, so I would pick that one too. In a matter of 10 min, my 2 choices were made, and I had completed what was expected of me, satisfied I didn't have to worry about it anymore. When the news of my acceptance in Biochemistry came, "Oh shit, what did I do?". Two and a half years later, I understood when my mom, who was trying to convince me to look into the chiropractic profession, mentioned she had met two chiropractic students studying for their biochemistry class at her chiropractor's open house. I knew this was the sign, a sign that I followed and that I am so happy I did.

- I have been married this year for 17 years. Of course, we've had ups and downs over the years, but even so, there have been many signs that he was my soul mate. My maiden name is Richard, his last name Wagner – Richard Wagner being a famous music composer. My brother and his older sister share the same birthdate, you can look at it as a fun coincidence, right? My half-brother (30+ younger than me) and his younger sister share the same birthday too. Too much coincidence here to keep calling them a coincidence.

Learn to recognize synchronicities in your life. Deepak Chopra said "Coincidences are clues from the Universe". When you live your life with an appreciation of coincidences and their meanings, you connect with the underlying field of infinite possibilities. This is when the magic begins, and when it becomes possible to achieve the spontaneous fulfillment of our every desire.

Exercise 12: Journal synchronicities as you see them occurring.

Here are 3 actions offered by Deepak Chopra to activate synchronicity and recognize the magic of life:

#1. Pay attention to each incident. Look at it. Hold it in your mind. Don't simply dismiss a coincidence and let it drift away. Life is totally interconnected. These unusual "things" are simply connections that surprise you because you aren't used to seeing life except in fragments. Now it is beginning to piece itself together. Journaling and keeping track of "what is" (step 1 of Activating your Life), is a good way to pay attention to synchronicity.

#2. Give significance to your experiences. This means changing your allegiance to a new way of perceiving yourself. You are accustomed to be an isolated person, bound by limited thoughts, feelings and experiences. This is the state of separation. Yet if you choose to, you can see yourself as part of the flow of life, the center of an unfolding, expanding awareness.

#3. Value this new way of being in the world. You are the silent, unchanging witness in the midst of constant change. The real you can comprehend far more than the limited self in separation. As you take your first steps into expanded consciousness, trust that the path is right, but don't trust every little incident.

3. Celebrating our wins.

I am noticing that a lot of people forget to recognize and celebrate what they have accomplished. It is so easy to focus on what we don't have, what we didn't get done, what we failed to do. Very often, we don't recognize what we have accomplished. On a normal day, I have 10-20 items on my to do list, from taking care of the house (feedings, cleaning, …), taking care of myself (working out, my hour of power, …), spending time with the people I love (kids, husband, family and friends), to work (clients, book, project, …). It is rare that I get through everything on my list, though I make priorities and accomplish what I can, focusing at the end of the day on being happy and satisfied with everything I was able to accomplish.

Bill Carmody, a successful CEO says the following: "When you celebrate, endorphins are released inside your body and you feel incredible. When you accomplish something and don't take the time to celebrate, you are robbing yourself of an important feeling that reinforces your success. Celebrating your wins not only feels great physically, but it reinforces the behavior you want to show up when you face a new challenge or opportunity."

Activating your Life by celebrating your wins aren't just about celebrating the *big* win. They're about celebrating the small wins. You will feel your life turn around as your mind gets excited about winning. Every time you celebrate, you rewire your brain, you activate your life for success. You'll want to challenge yourself and you'll be more likely to try harder things because you *celebrated* the smaller things.

Exercise 13: Use these three actions to build momentum.

#1: Create a Reflection schedule. Schedule weekly time-blocks where you intentionally think about your week. This time allows you to see your success and plan your next moves.

#2. Feel the win. Relive it, feel it, and integrate it – that's the secret formula. Remember, allowing your emotions to be expressed helps you rewire your brain for success, a key to Activating your Life.

#3. Share the win with others. Telling other people what you're proud of. Share what you're doing in your life with real enthusiasm. Being wild and excited about what you are doing and voicing it to the world is a way to show your motivation to the universe and it also helps you be accountable.

What if I fail?

I love this quote by **Michael Jordan:** "I've missed more than 9000 shots in my career. I've lost almost 300 games. 26 times, I've been trusted to take the game winning shot and missed. I've failed over and over and over again in my life. And that is why I succeed."

Failure is a part of life, of getting better and of winning. Failing is a sign that you are vulnerable, no one wins all the time. There can be plenty of reasons why. Getting clarity on what's you want to create and working on yourself is key to not allowing your mistake or your fear of failing hold you back.

The point of this book and my work is to help you figure out how to Activate your Life, how to shatter your unwanted habits, reprogram your body to live a healthy, good, successful Life.

Wrapping it all up!

To be shattering your habits and letting go of the old patterns, breaking them in such small pieces that the "old you" never comes back, you must understand and master these 7 principles. You must harmonize your physical, emotional, mind and soul. There is a lot of information in this book and, if you haven't realized, each principle is an affirmation.

In principle 1, "I see what is", I acknowledge where I start from and recognize what is my motivation (pain, bliss or inner guidance) and I learn to use my emotions to connect to my authentic self.

In principle 2, "I choose my destination", I set in my GPS (my mind) a goal. Dream goals and SMART goals are two key components to drive us forward.

In principle 3, "I am a spiritual being on a physical journey", I recognize that I am more than my body, my body is my vessel that carries my soul. Understanding the different aspects of my energetic being allows me to see how magical I truly am.

In principle 4, "I increase my adaptability", I understand how proper nutrition, exercise and regulating my nervous system allows me to have resources for reaching my goals.

In principle 5, "I repair my body", I recognize that my vessel (body) got beat up and I seek help to repair it. Repairing is one of the innate capacities of our amazing body.

In principle 6, "I change my thought, I change my life", by gaining knowledge and developing a curious and critical mind, I can rewire my own brain creating a glorious cycle to allow more Joy in my life.

In principle 7, "I follow up on myself", I see the importance of recognizing what season I am in, that synchronicities are clues from the universe, and I remember to celebrate my success.

You exist, you matter! There is only one of you that will ever exist, your uniqueness is a precious gift. By Activating your Life, you allow your light to shine brighter on this planet, and it will help you harness your power to produce new and powerful outcomes.

The world needs your light to shine.

"Don't ask yourself what the world needs; ask yourself what makes you come alive. And then go and do that. Because what the world needs are people who have come alive." - Harold Thurman

ABOUT THE AUTHOR

Dr. Emma Wagner, D.C. considers herself a child of the world, having lived in various countries in Africa, in France and in the United States. For over 25 years she has been passionately learning about the power of the mind and the adaptability of the physical body. Dr. Emma graduated a Doctor of Chiropractic in 2000, and since then she has helped thousands in her private.

Know that I am here to help you, and that I would love to help you. Here are different ways to stay in touch and get the help and guidance that you need:

- Learn more about me   www.DrEmmaWagner.com

- Email your questions or comments to emmawagnerhealer@gmail.com

- Connect with me on Facebook @dremmawagner

- Visit me in my office in San Clemente, CA.

Made in the USA
Middletown, DE
13 July 2023